# We Need Water

## by Helen Frost

Consulting Editor: Gail Saunders-Smith, Ph.D.

Reviewer: Carolyn M. Tucker
Water Education Specialist
California Department of Water Resources

## Pebble Books

an imprint of Capstone Press
Mankato, Minnesota

Pebble Books are published by Capstone Press
151 Good Counsel Drive, P.O. Box 669, Mankato, Minnesota 56002
http://www.capstone-press.com

2  3  4  5  6  7  07  06  05  04  03  02

Library of Congress Cataloging-in-Publication Data
Frost, Helen, 1949–
    We need water / by Helen Frost.
    p. cm.—(Water)
    Includes bibliographical references (p. 23) and index.
    Summary: Briefly outlines some of the many reasons that water is necessary for
life, from growing plants, cooking food, and washing things to staying cool.
    ISBN 0-7368-0413-7 (hardcover)
    ISBN 0-7368-8638-9 (paperback)
    1. Water—Juvenile literature. [1. Water.] I. Title. II. Series: Frost, Helen,
1949– Water.
GB662.3F764 2000
533.7—dc21
                                                                99-19591

# Note to Parents and Teachers

The Water series supports national science standards for
understanding the properties of water. This book describes and
illustrates ways people, plants, and animals need and use water.
The photographs support early readers in understanding the text.
The repetition of words and phrases helps early readers learn new
words. This book also introduces early readers to subject-specific
vocabulary words, which are defined in the Words to Know section.
Early readers may need assistance to read some words and to use
the Table of Contents, Words to Know, Read More, Internet Sites,
and Index/Word List sections of the book.

# Table of Contents

Water and Life . . . . . . . . . . . 5

Using Water . . . . . . . . . . . 15

Words to Know . . . . . . . . . 22

Read More . . . . . . . . . . . 23

Internet Sites . . . . . . . . . . . 23

Index/Word List . . . . . . . . . 24

All living things
need water.

Animals need water to live. Some animals drink water from rivers and lakes.

Plants need water
to live. Plants use
water in the ground.

Some plants and animals live in water. Seaweed grows in water. Fish swim in water.

People need water
to live. People need to
drink water every day.

People need water
to grow food. Farmers
use water to grow crops
and raise animals.

People need water to cook. Boiling water cooks food.

18

People need water to wash. People wash their bodies and clothes with water.

People need water
to stay cool.

# Words to Know

**boil**—to heat water or another liquid until it bubbles; boiling water cooks food.

**crop**—a plant grown in large amounts; crops usually are grown for food; farmers use water to grow crops.

**lake**—a large body of water that is surrounded by land; most lakes are freshwater lakes.

**river**—a large stream of freshwater that flows into a lake or an ocean; most of the water people use every day comes from rivers.

**seaweed**—a plant that grows underwater

# Read More

Collard, Sneed B. *Our Wet World: Exploring Earth's Aquatic Ecosystems.* Watertown, Mass.: Charlesbridge, 1998.

Hooper, Meredith. *The Drop in My Drink: The Story of Water on Our Planet.* New York: Viking, 1998.

Valat, Pierre-Marie. *Water.* A First Discovery Book. New York: Cartwheel Books, 1996.

# Internet Sites

**Clean Water Clear Choice—Fun Facts**
http://www.cleanwaterclearchoice.org/kids/facts.html

**Everyone Needs Water**
http://www.nwf.org/kids/cool/water1.html

**Home Water Usage**
http://www.ci.arlington.tx.us/waterdice/homewaterusage.html

**Water Water Everywhere**
http://www.beesinc.org/resource/currenha/curewate.htm

# Index/Word List

animals, 7,
 11, 15
bodies, 19
boiling, 17
clothes, 19
cook, 17
cool, 21
crops, 15
drink, 7, 13
farmers, 15

fish, 11
food, 15, 17
ground, 9
grow, 11, 15
lakes, 7
live, 7, 9,
 11, 13
need, 5, 7, 9,
 13, 15, 17,
 19, 21

people, 13,
 15, 17,
 19, 21
plants, 9, 11
raise, 15
rivers, 7
seaweed, 11
swim, 11
wash, 19

**Word Count: 99**
**Early-Intervention Level: 13**

**Editorial Credits**
Mari C. Schuh, editor; Timothy Halldin, cover designer; Kimberly Danger,
 photo researcher

**Photo Credits**
ColePhoto/John S. Reid, 18
Frances M. Roberts, 8
Index Stock Imagery, cover
Inga Spence/TOM STACK & ASSOCIATES, 14
Jack Glisson, 16
Photo Network/Mark Sherman, 10; Peter Fownes, 12
Photophile/Thomas Arledge, 20
Robert McCaw, 6
Unicorn Stock Photos/Robin Rudd, 1; Ed Harp, 4

**NON F**
**FRO**
**1.2**

Frost, Helen
  We Need Water
          $15.99

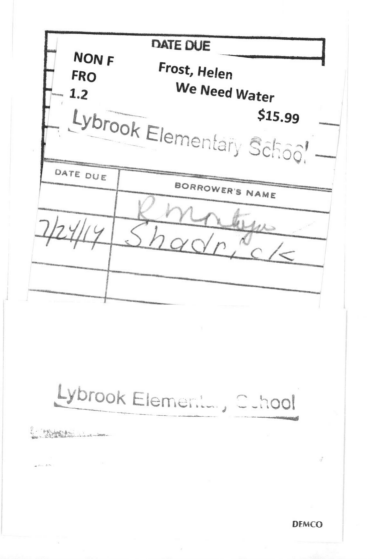

| DATE DUE | |
|---|---|

**NON F**
**FRO**
**1.2**

Frost, Helen
  We Need Water
          $15.99

| DATE DUE | BORROWER'S NAME |
|---|---|
| 7/24/14 | R M___ Shadrick |
| | |
| | |

DEMCO